ALL ABOUT

Energy

ELLA NEWELL

raintree

a Capstone company — publishers for children

Raintree is an imprint of Capstone Global Library Limited, a company incorporated in England and Wales having its registered office at 264 Banbury Road, Oxford, OX2 7DY – Registered company number: 6695582

www.raintree.co.uk
myorders@raintree.co.uk

ISBN 978 1 4747 7718 6 (hardback)
ISBN 978 1 4747 7725 4 (paperback)

British Library Cataloguing in Publication Data
A full catalogue record for this book is available from the British Library.

Acknowledgements
We would like to thank the following for permission to reproduce photographs:
Cover: Shutterstock: Vaclav Volrab. Inside: Dreamstime: Mark Fairey 7; NASA: 11; Shutterstock: Rich Carey 45, Jacek Chabraszewski 4, Chrisbrignell 40, Tad Denson 42, Charlie Edward 38, Iakov Filimonov 27, Marco Gerodetti 17, Jason and Bonnie Grower 43, Craig Hanson 22-23, Holdeneye 44, IM Photo 14, Imging 26, Jag CZ 32, Cris Kelly 28, Koi88 23t, Karol Kozlowski 24, David P. Lewis 37r, Torsten Lorenz 15, Marquisphoto 20, N.Minton 34, Monkey Business Images 10, Nejron Photo 8, Nexus 7 13, Nito 19, Presniakov Oleksandr 18, Pavel L Photo and Video 9, Phovoir 41, Dr. Morley Read 39, Wyatt Rivard 25, Huguette Roe 33, Tangencial 28-29, Ttstudio 21, Tupungato 31, Vibrant Image Studio 16, Viktoriya 5, Anthony Jay D. Villalon 35, Wavebreakmedia 6, Poznukhov Yuriy 12, ZoranOrcik 1, 36-37; Wikimedia Commons: P123 30.

Every effort has been made to contact copyright holders of material reproduced in this book. Any omissions will be rectified in subsequent printings if notice is given to the publisher.

Contents

Energy everywhere

Energy is everywhere but it is invisible. It makes things happen. Energy is the ability to make things work. This book will tell you about different types of energy, where they come from, what they do and how they work.

Useful energy

Nothing works without energy – not even our bodies! Energy comes from different sources and in different shapes and sizes. Some sources of energy, such as the Sun, provide endless amounts of energy that we can trap and use directly, or use to create other energy sources. Others, such as a flash of lightning in the sky, are very difficult to trap and do not provide enough energy to make trapping them worthwhile.

You use energy for everything you do, from riding a bike to phoning a friend.

All about matter

Energy is found in atoms. Atoms are the incredibly tiny particles that make up everything in the universe – including us! They are the building blocks of everything that exists in the world. They are so tiny you can see them only if you use a very powerful microscope. One hundred million atoms would only cover your fingernail! Atoms join together to make molecules.

LIFE WITHOUT ENERGY

Without energy, nothing would exist, not even our planet, Earth. Scientists believe that all the energy in the world started with the Big Bang. About 13 billion years ago, a tiny speck of matter that contained all the energy and matter that has ever existed exploded and created our universe.

Chapter One

All about energy

Everything we do uses energy, from eating breakfast to running for a bus or reading a book. Everything we use depends on energy. Computers, lights and heaters all need energy to work. Energy is everywhere!

Types of energy

Scientists believe that energy cannot be created or destroyed. However, it can be turned from one type of energy into another.

The different types of energy include:

- thermal or heat energy such as a flame that heats a saucepan
- kinetic or movement energy such as a spinning wheel
- light energy such as the Sun's light
- Sound energy such as your voice travelling
- Electrical energy such as a socket and plug powering a computer
- Chemical energy such as energy stored in food.

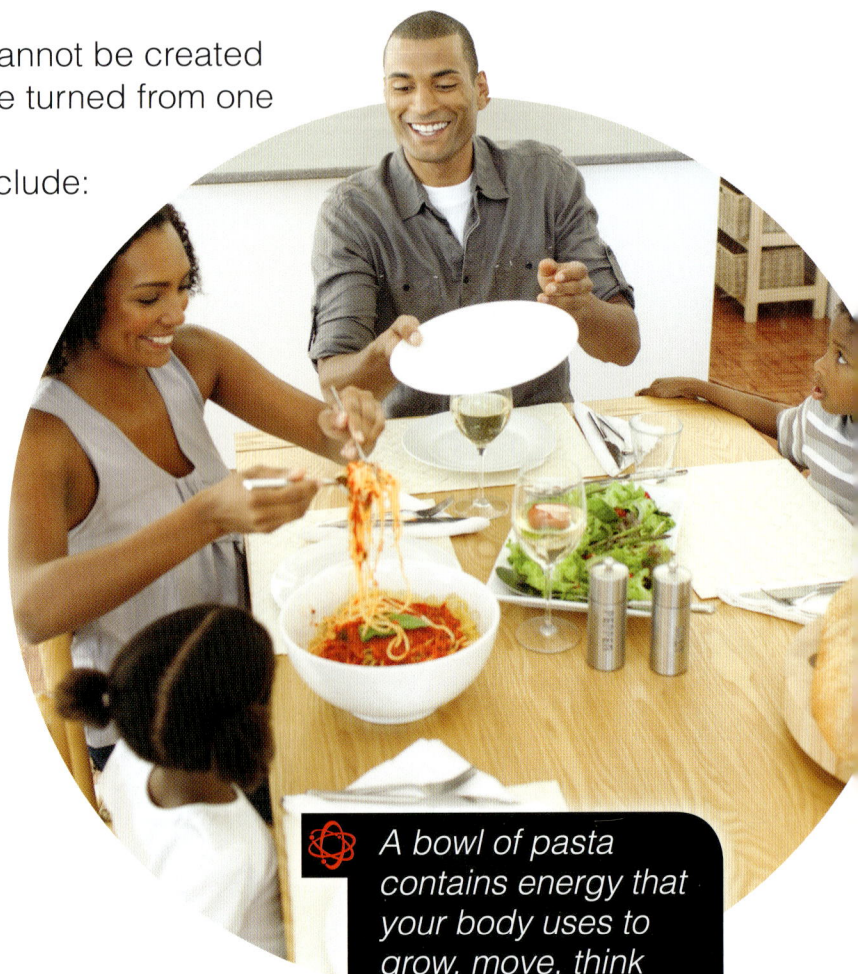

A bowl of pasta contains energy that your body uses to grow, move, think and repair itself.

When you stretch an elastic band, the energy stored in the elastic band is waiting to spring back. This is called potential energy. It is energy just waiting to be used.

Sunny source

The blazing Sun is the source of most of our energy. Without the Sun's energy, there would be no plants, no food and no life.

Photosynthesis

Green plants soak up light energy from the Sun. This light energy is stored in the plant via a process called photosynthesis. When animals eat plants, the plants' stored energy gives them energy to grow.

Energy and us

Energy keeps us alive. Tiny amounts of electrical energy send messages from the brain to our nerves. Chemical energy helps our bodies break down food, so we can use the stores of energy in food to keep fit and healthy.

Potential energy is stored in this elastic band.

Light and sound

When we talk to our friends, sound energy carries our voices. When we step outside our homes in the morning, light energy makes it possible for us to see where we are going.

Let there be light

Light is a form of travelling energy. The light we can see is visible light. It is one type of light in the electromagnetic spectrum. Light is made up of waves of electromagnetic radiation. The waves are made up of billions of tiny packets or particles of energy called photons. As far as scientists know, light is the fastest thing in the universe – one particle of light takes 100,000 years to travel from one side of the galaxy to the other.

Light from the Sun reaches Earth in about eight minutes.

When you listen to music, you are hearing sound energy.

Waves of sound

Sound is energy. When you make a noise, invisible vibrations (waves of sound) travel through the air. When something vibrates, tiny parts of the air, called particles, move. As the particles move and bump into other particles, more particles are bumped. It is like one domino falling and knocking over all the other dominoes in a line. The bumping, moving particles are sound waves. Our ears hear them as sound.

SUPER SCIENCE FACT

As sound contains only a small amount of energy, it is not often used to make things work. However, scientists are looking for new methods with which to use energy from sound. For example, sound energy from a human voice could recharge mobile phones. Sound could be turned into electricity, so that mobiles could be powered while we talk on them!

Hot, hot, hot

On a hot sunny day, the Sun's rays warm the air. On a cold day, we wear coats to keep warm. The warmth of the Sun and the warmth trapped by our clothes is heat (thermal) energy.

Layers of clothes trap the body's heat energy, keeping you warm.

Heat on the move

Atoms are always moving, shaking and vibrating. When they are heated, they vibrate faster. This creates heat energy. Heat energy moves from a warm place to a cool place. When it moves through gas or liquids, it is called convection. The movement of heat through materials is called conduction. Heat energy can change a substance from one state to another. When solid ice is warmed, it turns to liquid water. If this is boiled, it turns to steam.

Great ball of fire

The Sun is a burning ball of heat and gases. Invisible rays of heat energy from the Sun travel across space to Earth as electromagnetic waves called radiation. We feel the Sun's heat as radiation. Unlike convection and conduction, radiation does not transfer heat energy through moving atoms.

SUPER SCIENCE FACT

As people move around, they give off heat energy. This heat can be used to help keep buildings warm. For example, in the Mall of Minneapolis, Minnesota, USA, special machines called heat exchangers have been installed. These machines use the human heat energy given off by shoppers to heat water. The hot water is then used to heat the shopping mall!

11

All change

Energy can be converted (changed) from one form to another. For example, your computer is powered by electrical energy. But that electrical energy comes from heat energy made in a power station where fuel is burned to produce electricity.

Electricity is made by converting other sources of energy, such as coal, into electrical energy.

Lots of power

Huge amounts of energy are converted into electrical energy in a power station. Here, a fuel, such as coal, is burned to heat water. The water boils, and turns into steam. The steam turns the heat energy from the burning fuel into kinetic energy. The kinetic energy turns blades on a turbine, which power a generator. The generator turns energy from the moving blades into current electricity. The force from the power station sends the electrical energy to where it is needed.

Changing energy

Different types of energy are used to make a car move. It all starts when the driver starts the ignition. This triggers the car's battery to release chemical energy that turns into electrical energy. The electrical energy provides a spark that burns fuel and air so the car can move.

Petrol and diesel are packed with energy from crude oil.

It's electric

About 200 years ago, people lived without televisions, telephones, air conditioning, computers and light bulbs. They lived without electrical energy, but today electrical energy has transformed the world in which we live.

Electric electrons

Atoms consist of tiny particles called protons, neutrons and electrons. The protons and neutrons gather together in the nucleus (centre) of the atom. The electrons are free to move around the atom. Electricity is an invisible form of energy that is stored in electrons and protons. A current of electricity is a steady flow of electrons around a circuit – an unbroken path through which electricity can flow. Heat energy is often used to force the movement of electrons.

On and off

The current of electricity we can turn on and off at the flick of a switch usually comes from power stations. It will not run out as long as the power stations are able to keep producing electrical energy.

Night and day, massive amounts of electricity light up cities and towns around the world.

Store and charge

Batteries are stores of electrical energy. When the battery's circuit is closed, a chemical mixture or paste creates electrons. These flow through the battery to provide electrical energy. When the battery is "flat" it means that all its stored energy has been used up.

Batteries are portable packs of energy.

SUPER SCIENCE FACT

Electric eels can blast their prey with 600 volts of electricity. Thousands of cells in the eel's body, called electrocytes, store power like tiny batteries. An aquarium in Japan created a device that used an eel's electrical energy to power the lights on a Christmas tree!

15

Chapter Two
Energy sources

From the shining Sun to sticky oil at the bottom of the sea, energy comes from different sources. You can touch and feel some energy sources that are taken from the ground, such as coal. You cannot touch others such as the wind. Their energy has to be caught, or harnessed, in order to use it.

We use energy sources that formed millions of years ago under the sea and deep beneath Earth.

Rich old energy

Coal, oil and natural gas are called fossil fuels. They formed from the remains of plants and animals over millions of years. Some of the plant remains formed coal, while others formed oil and natural gas.

Releasing energy

Fossil fuels contain energy-rich groups of atoms called hydrocarbons. When the fuels are burned, they release energy. These energy sources are non-renewable. They cannot be replaced, and will eventually run out.

Rotten creatures

Oil and natural gas come from the remains of small creatures and plants found in water. These creatures and plants were buried under the ocean or in rivers, and covered by mud, sand and rocks. The weight and heat of the sand and other materials pressed down on the rotting creatures and plants, taking away any air, and converting the remains into oil and natural gas. Gas formed nearer the surface of Earth, and oil formed further under the ground.

The natural environment is rich in sources of energy.

Buried energy

Coal formed millions of years ago, but it still contains the energy that once lived in the plants from which it formed. When coal is burned, the plants' old energy is released. Coal burns easily, releasing lots of energy, but it also releases many gases and leaves behind ash.

Rotten plants

Millions of years ago, leaves, trees, bark, roots and dying plants lay on the surface of Earth. Layers of this rotting plant matter were covered by soil, sand and water, turning it to peat. Over thousands of years, heat and pressure from the top layers pressed on the peat. Hard rocks formed over the peat, squeezing out any water, eventually turning it to coal. In some countries, peat is used as an energy source.

Ancient plants continue to provide the energy to power modern society.

Dig deep

Coal is taken out of the ground (extracted) by mining. Some mining involves shovelling coal from near Earth's surface. There are different types of coal, depending on the pressure and heat on the coal as it formed. Each type contains different amounts of energy. The energy in coal is measured in British Thermal Units (Btus). Around 450 grams (1 pound) of coal from Colorado, USA, contains enough energy – about 10,000 Btus – to make five pots of coffee.

LIFE WITHOUT COAL

What would our world be like if we ran out of coal? Coal is used to create around 30 per cent of the UK's electricity, but many of the manufactured goods we buy are created in China, a country that requires huge amounts of coal for its industries. If China did not have coal, we would be without many of the appliances we use in our everyday lives.

The largest reserves of coal are found in the United States, China, Russia and India.

19

Oil and gas

Natural gas and oil are fossil fuels. Natural gas is invisible, colourless, shapeless and odourless. It is made up of several chemicals and gases. The main gas is methane. Oil is dark and sticky. It is found deep on the ocean floor, where it formed millions of years ago from the remains of sea animals and plants.

Getting the gas

Geologists work out where there are large amounts of natural gas. Then, engineers drill massive holes, called wells, in the ground. The natural gas seeps into the wells. It is then carried through pipes to a refinery where it is cleaned to get rid of any unwanted material. A network of pipes carries the gas directly to houses and businesses, or to power stations, where it is used to create electrical energy. A chemical is added to natural gas to make it smell. This is a safety measure, so that we can tell when gas has leaked into the air. Natural gas is very flammable, which means it burns easily.

After natural gas is extracted, it has to be processed before it can be used.

Driven on oil

Crude oil is the raw oil taken from the bottom of the ocean floor. The raw oil is transported to a refinery. The refinery is made up of huge towers where the oil is passed through many processes to turn it into the petrol that powers cars, buses and other vehicles.

Hundreds of football pitches could fit inside an oil refinery!

LIFE WITHOUT OIL

In the 1800s people discovered how to separate oil into different chemicals by refining it. Kerosene was then used to light lamps and petrol was used as fuel for cars. The increasing demand for cars, lorries, trains and aeroplanes led to a huge demand for fuel. That demand continues today.

Atomic power

Nuclear energy is energy stored in the centre of an atom. To release this energy, atoms in a metal called uranium are split apart. This takes place in a nuclear power station in a process called nuclear fission.

About three-quarters of France's power comes from nuclear energy.

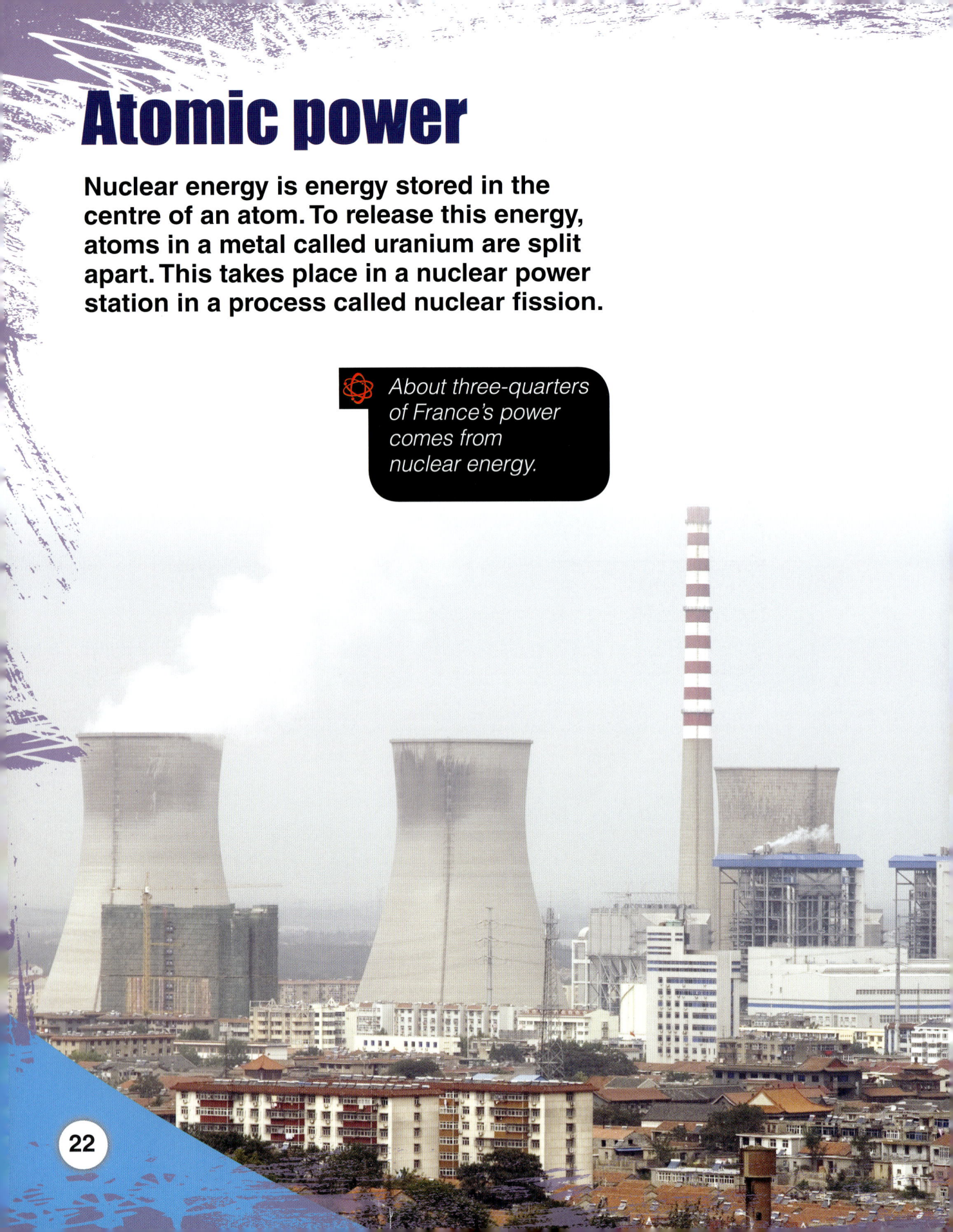

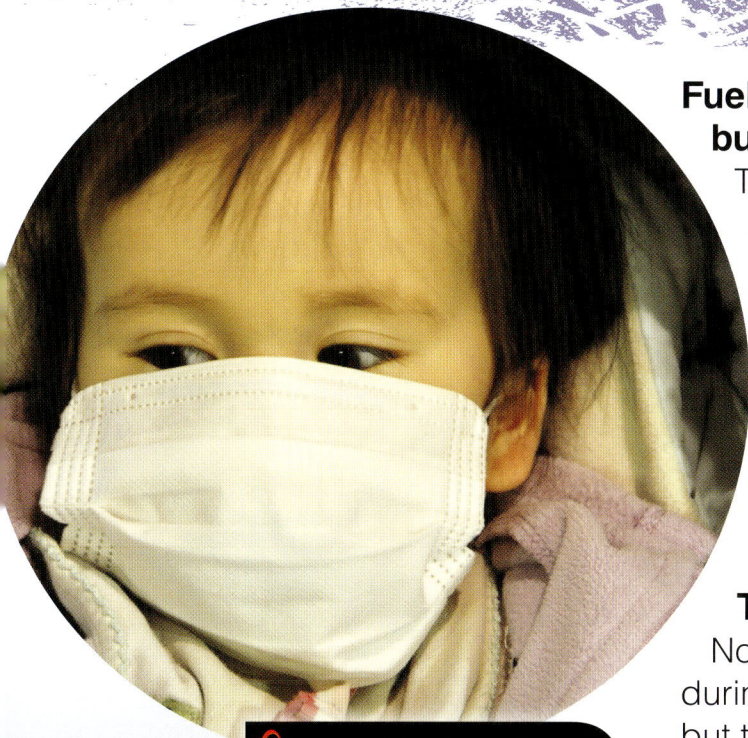

Fuel without burning

The atoms in uranium are easy to split. In a nuclear reactor, special rods are used to break up the atoms in uranium. The energy from this is then used to heat water. The heat energy from the water creates steam, which in turn powers a generator to make electricity.

Leaks of nuclear materials cause great harm to people, animals and the natural environment.

The good and the bad

No harmful gases are released during the production of nuclear fuel, but there are other harmful effects. Uranium is radioactive. This means it gives off invisible rays of energy that can be very dangerous. Radioactivity released from creating nuclear power is extremely strong and can be deadly. No one has found a safe way to get rid of the radioactive waste left by nuclear power stations. It is also difficult to control leaks of radioactive material from nuclear power stations. In 2011, a tsunami swamped the Japanese Fukushima nuclear power station and led to leaks of radioactive material.

SUPER SCIENCE FACT

Nuclear power stations use a small amount of fuel. About 1 kilogram (2.4 pounds) of uranium produce as much energy as around 3,000 tonnes of coal.

Burning problems

Fossil fuels and nuclear power provide about 93 per cent of the world's energy. Using these energy sources damages the environment. Burning fossil fuels releases harmful gases and adds to pollution. Extracting fossil fuels and uranium from deep beneath Earth's surface destroys the surrounding area and habitats.

Chemicals released from burning fossil fuels cause acid rain. This seeps into the soil and destroys the leaves on trees.

Greenhouse gases

Burning coal releases a lot of useful energy but it also releases carbon dioxide. Carbon dioxide is called a greenhouse gas because it traps heat in Earth's atmosphere. Earth needs a certain amount of heat for everything to survive, but too much heat has led to global warming. Global warming is having dramatic and damaging effects on the world's weather patterns. Natural gas releases less carbon dioxide than coal, but a lot of methane escapes into the atmosphere from natural gas wells and pipelines. Methane traps heat in Earth's atmosphere, adding to global warming.

Fracking

New methods are being used to extract natural gas from hard rocks called shale. This type of extraction has released huge amounts of gas, supplying a quarter of the United States' natural gas supplies. To extract natural gas, small explosions shatter the rock and high pressure forces fluids underground. This is called fracking. Some scientists believe this process disturbs Earth's structure and can trigger earthquakes. People who live near fracking sites have reported poisoned water and other environmental problems.

SUPER SCIENCE FACT

Scientists believe that global warming is melting the frozen waters of the Arctic. As the ice melts, sea levels rise. Species are left without their habitats or food sources. The effect cannot be reversed.

Chapter Three
Renewable sources

Nature is packed with limitless energy sources such as the wind.

Fossil fuels are in limited supply and burning them releases harmful amounts of carbon dioxide into the atmosphere. To meet the world's growing energy needs, we need energy sources that will not run out. These are called renewable energy sources. Electricity itself is neither renewable nor non-renewable, but the fuels that are used to create electricity can be renewable (such as sunlight) or non-renewable (such as coal).

Renewable sources

The wind blows, rivers flow and the Sun shines. These natural forces supply endless amounts of energy. These sources are sometimes called "green" energy because they are less harmful to the environment than fossil fuels.

Planting trees to replace those chopped down for fuel makes wood renewable.

Why renew?

Renewable energy is clean, and it will not run out. However, renewable energy does not always provide enough energy to meet everyone's needs. It can also be very expensive to set up. Machines and devices to harness energy from the wind or water can disturb natural environments and habitats.

Renewable or not?

Wood can be used as a fuel. This is only renewable if trees are planted to replace the wood burned for fuel. The trees will grow within our human time frame. Coal is made from dead plants and animals. However, it is not renewable because it takes millions of years to form. Biomass is a fuel from plant matter such as crops. It is only renewable if plants or crops are grown to replace those used for energy.

LIFE WITHOUT OIL, GAS AND COAL

Some scientists say there is enough oil left for just 50 years, natural gas for 70 years and coal for about 100 years. They believe we will use 35 per cent more energy in 20 years' time, because the world's population is growing so fast and more people use more energy. According to some estimates, renewable energy provides about 13 per cent of the energy used around the world. This figure needs to increase in order for us to provide enough energy for the future.

27

The Sun's energy

Earth receives more energy from the Sun in one hour than the whole world uses in the same amount of time. Scientists are always looking for ways to store the Sun's energy so that it can be used at night and during the day, and in all weather conditions.

Catch it!

Solar cells (also called photovoltaic cells) turn the Sun's energy into electrical energy. Materials in the cells, called semiconductors, soak up photons of light and release electrons. The electrons create electricity. Single cells create enough electricity to power a watch or calculator, but thousands of solar cells on large panels create enough electricity to light and heat houses and businesses.

The Sun's heat can be used to cook a meal on a solar oven.

Computer-guided mirrors, called heliostats, focus sunlight onto a central tower, to heat up water and drive steam turbines.

Sun power

At a solar power station, specially shaped mirrors focus hot sunlight onto long pipes filled with oil. The boiling liquid travels down pipes to heat water into steam. This is used to turn a generator to create electricity. It works in the same way as a power station that uses fossil fuels but no fuel is burned, so it is not as harmful to the environment.

Energy for everyone

Solar power is very useful in sunny, remote parts of the world where it is often too expensive or difficult to use electrical cables. In these areas, solar power is used to run many everyday things, such as fridges or computers.

SUPER SCIENCE FACT

Cars made up of panels of photovoltaic cells use sunshine for fuel. A back-up battery stores the Sun's energy and releases it when it is needed. You probably won't see many of these cars on the road because they are very expensive to produce.

Wet and windy!

The wind will always blow and water will always flow. The kinetic energy in wind and flowing water can be turned into clean, renewable electrical energy.

Wind works

Thermal energy from the Sun causes currents, which create wind. To use the wind's energy, wind turbines are linked to a generator. When the wind blows, it transfers kinetic energy, and turns huge blades mounted on a tall tower. The blades turn and drive the generator, creating electricity. However, the wind's energy lasts only while the wind blows.

Energetic water

Waves, tides and rivers are all energy sources. Wave-power machines on the shore or in the sea turn wave energy into electricity. A wave farm can power 62,000 homes but it is hard to build the machines in stormy seas. Twice a day, the sea sweeps massive amounts of water across the shore. This tidal movement can be used to create electrical energy.

This huge machine turns the kinetic energy from waves into electricity. The power travels in cables under the sea to land.

People have been using wind power for thousands of years. Wind has been used to power sailing ships. Wind turned farmers' mills to grind wheat and pump water. Today, huge wind farms are found on land and at sea all over the world.

Hydroelectricity

Hydroelectric power is the energy from flowing water. As water flows, a turbine turns the water's kinetic energy into mechanical energy. This makes the turbine spin at a high speed, driving a generator that converts the mechanical energy into electrical energy.

Hydroelectric power provides about 60 per cent of Austria's electricity.

A load of bio!

Biomass is decaying plant or animal matter and organic matter such as wood or crops. Biomass is a renewable energy source as long as crops or trees are planted to replace those used for fuel.

Burning bio

When burned, the chemical energy in biomass is released as heat. Wood chips, waste or crops are burned to create steam for making electricity, or to provide heat. Biomass can be turned into other forms of energy such as gas or fuels. Some cars run on the oil used to cook food!

Give and take

Biomass contains stored energy from the Sun. When biomass is burned, this energy is released as heat. In the same way that burning fossil fuels releases carbon dioxide, so does burning biomass. However, the biomass soaks up carbon dioxide when it grows.

Cow dung contains a gas called methane. This gas can power a machine that makes electricity.

Sweden uses so much rubbish for renewable energy that it has to import rubbish from other countries to meet the demand.

SUPER SCIENCE FACT

The average US household throws away more than 2 kilograms (4 pounds) of rubbish every day. If all the rubbish in the United States was converted to energy, it could power a city the size of Buffalo, New York, for one year. An average kitchen-sized rubbish bag contains enough energy to light a 100-watt light bulb for more than 20 hours.

Hot Earth!

Deep inside Earth, it is even hotter than the surface of the Sun! Geothermal energy is the heat inside Earth. Sometimes, geothermal energy bursts out of the ground in the form of volcanoes or hot springs. Geothermal is renewable because Earth's core is always hot.

Earth's inner heat will last forever, making it an extremely useful source of energy.

Hot inside!

The inside of Earth is made up of layers. The core at the centre is made of iron. This is surrounded by hot molten rock, called magma. The outer layer, called the crust, can be more than 48 kilometres (30 miles) thick, and is made up of plates that fit together like puzzle pieces. Underground, the magma heats rocks and water. Boiling magma pushes through at the edges of the plates and bursts out of the surface where volcanoes occur.

Taking the heat

Water from deep inside Earth is heated by geothermal energy. To use the energy, water or steam is pumped from deep wells. Hot water near Earth's surface can be used directly for heat by being pumped into buildings.

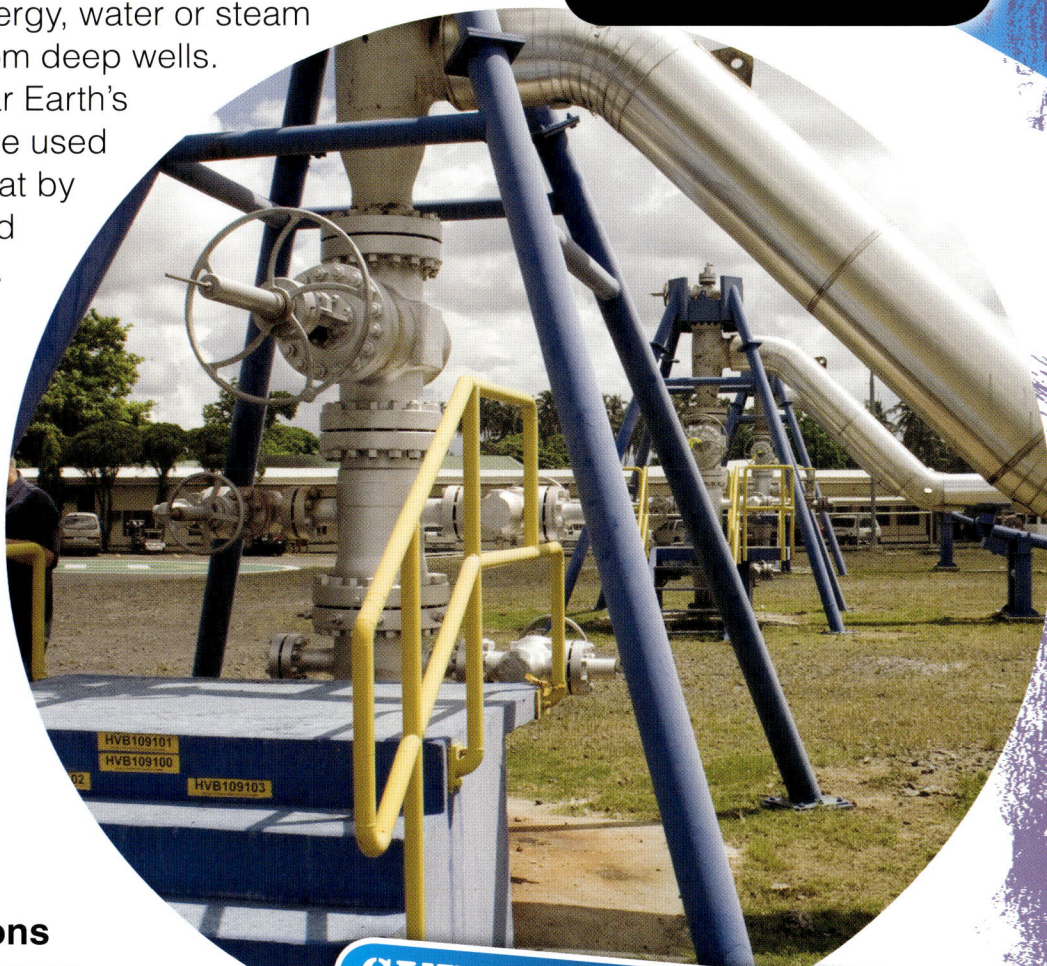

Power stations

Geothermal power stations use the steam from geothermal reservoirs (large areas with geothermal energy near the surface of Earth) to power a turbine. Others use the hot water to boil fluid that turns into steam and then turns a turbine. No fuel is burned, so no harmful gases are released.

SUPER SCIENCE FACT

American Indians used hot springs for cooking 10,000 years ago. Today, many buildings in Iceland, a country with a lot of volcanoes, are heated with geothermal hot water.

35

Chapter Four
Today's energy

The more energy we use, the more pollution we create. Scientists face a difficult balancing act as they try to find cleaner energy sources to meet the growing demand, and find more ways to reduce energy use.

Energy wars

As supplies are running out and demand is growing, energy is a hot topic. Governments can make a lot of money by selling their energy resources to other countries. Governments can also use energy resources as a means to get what they want. For example, Russia is a gas-rich country. In 2009, it cut off gas sent through pipes in Ukraine because of a dispute over the price paid for the gas. This led to a drop in gas supplies in other European countries, and to some blackouts.

Countries want to protect their crucial energy supplies.

Powerless

Using too much energy can lead to a blackout, or power failure. In July 2012, the city of Delhi, India, experienced one of the world's worst electrical blackouts. More than 670 million people were affected as the supply of electricity stopped. Miners were stranded underground as lifts stopped working, trains stopped running and lights went out. It is believed that the blackout may have been caused by a combination of a lack of electricity from hydroelectric dams because of low rainfall, and extremely high demand for electricity.

Gas use is measured by meters. People have to pay for the energy that they use.

SUPER SCIENCE FACT

One of the first power stations in New York, USA, generated enough electricity to provide light in about 85 homes! In 1800, around 60,000 people lived in New York City. Today, around 8 million people live in the city – imagine how much power must be created every day to light their homes!

37

Clean it up

In their raw state, coal and oil do not cause pollution. They are polluting and harmful to the environment only when they are burned to provide energy. Scientists are constantly working to find ways to make fossil fuels cleaner and to limit the damage caused to our planet by using these energy resources.

Weather patterns around the world are changing and becoming far less predictable.

Global warming

Our energy use has a huge effect on our planet. Too much carbon dioxide in the atmosphere has resulted in a rise in our planet's temperature (see pages 24–25) and also causes extreme weather conditions such as flooding.

Clean coal?

Coal is known as the dirtiest fossil fuel because it releases a lot of carbon dioxide when it is burned. Scientists are trying to limit the amount of carbon dioxide released. They are also trying to capture and store the carbon dioxide before it enters Earth's atmosphere.

Burning coal produces lots of ash. Scientists are looking at ways to use coal ash to make concrete tougher. Coal ash can also be used on bridges and roads to make them stronger.

Vast areas of precious rainforest have been cleared to grow crops that will be used for fuel.

Into the Amazon

Huge areas of the Amazon rainforest have been cut down or burned so that crops can be grown. The crops (such as sugar cane or oilseed) are processed to use as energy sources. But the trees that stood in the rainforest for thousands of years were important for soaking up greenhouse gases from all over the world. The forests were also home to thousands of insects and animals, as well as native people.

39

Saving energy

We cannot make new energy or destroy energy, so why do we need to save it? The answer is because of the harmful effect of burning fossil fuels and because lots of energy is "lost".

Lost energy

A glowing lamp releases heat energy that is hard to reuse. On a larger scale, coal-fired power stations lose about one-third of their heat energy when they make electricity. Heat energy is hard to use again or capture. The energy disappears into the atmosphere.

Using wind-up gadgets, such as this travel lamp, is a great way to save energy.

Recycle

It usually takes less energy to make something from recycled materials than it does to make it from new materials. Making a tonne of paper from recycled paper saves up to 17 trees and uses 50 per cent less water. Reusing objects means new ones do not have to be created, therefore saving energy. Engineers, architects and designers are always looking for new ways to design and build in an energy-efficient way.

Treading power

Your body is a powerhouse of energy! Scientists are increasingly interested in ways to "collect" small amounts of energy from movement and sound energy. Energy from a moving body can be turned into electrical energy. For example, special tiles have been created so that when a person steps on them, the kinetic energy from their body is turned into electrical energy. This energy is used to power lights.

Recycling saves energy used to create new products and limits the amount of rubbish in landfill sites.

SUPER SCIENCE FACT

A wind-up radio uses the energy from turning a rotor to create electrical energy. More and more products, such as torches, are being made that work in a similar way. These provide important, cheap energy sources.

41

Trapped!

To meet the world's growing energy needs, scientists are investigating ways to unlock energy from sources that they know contain large amounts of energy but are difficult to trap or get out of the ground.

Methane hydrates

Deep beneath the seabed, vast amounts of energy are trapped in cages of ice called methane hydrates. They contain huge amounts of methane, the main part of natural gas. These icy structures may contain more energy than all of the existing reserves of oil, coal and gas put together. They were created by natural processes in material deep beneath Earth. However, these energy sources can be very dangerous to harness and no one has yet discovered a safe way to get them from the bottom of the sea.

Although we currently mine for oil at the bottom of the ocean, no one has yet discovered a safe means by which to extract methane hydrates from the seabed.

Hydrogen fuel was used to power NASA's space shuttles.

Hydrogen

There is a lot of hydrogen in the world – in water, air and living things. Hydrogen is produced from other substances such as natural gas and water. It is packed with energy and can be burned to release heat energy. When used with a device called a fuel cell, it creates electricity. Apart from energy, the only thing hydrogen leaves behind is water. However, creating hydrogen from other sources uses up energy, which in turn creates carbon dioxide.

SUPER SCIENCE FACT

From the 1970s, NASA used hydrogen to power some of its space shuttles. Hydrogen fuel cells powered the shuttles' electrical systems. Creating energy in this way produced water, which the crew drank!

Tomorrow's energy

What will the energy sources of the future be? Scientists around the world are experimenting with and researching different energy sources. Some of our energy needs will be met by existing sources and some will need to be met by new discoveries.

Using poo!

Cow dung can be collected and heated in a tank that creates methane. This biogas can fuel a large engine to produce renewable electricity. As well as producing gas, this reduces the problem of what to do with animal waste. There is less odour from the dung, and waste from the process can be used as bedding for other animals.

Tomorrow's clean energy needs may be met by harnessing the power of rubbish or animal waste.

Algae produce energy by photosynthesis. Scientists extract the oil from algae, which contains energy, and convert it to usable fuel.

Green soup

Green slime called algae is powering some aircraft as well as soaking up unwanted carbon dioxide. This plant doubles in size every two hours, so it is renewable. It can grow in fresh water and does not need much space. It produces some carbon dioxide when it is burned, but soaks up lots, too. When the oil is taken out of the plant, the rest can be used to feed animals.

A lot of hot air?

A small company in the UK has created petrol from the carbon dioxide found in air and the hydrogen found in water. It may take many years to see if this is a realistic energy source that can be used in the future.

LIFE WITHOUT CLEANER RENEWABLE ENERGY

Unless we discover practical, clean, renewable energy sources, we will worsen the effect of pollution and global warming, and Earth will suffer. Our challenge is both to provide usable energy for everyone around the world and to protect the future of our planet.

Glossary

atom tiny pieces of matter that make up all life

biomass natural matter that is used for fuel

carbon dioxide colourless, odourless greenhouse gas that is found in the atmosphere and is given off when fossil fuels are burned

chemical energy energy made by the reaction of certain substances

circuit closed loop of wire through which a current of electricity flows

convert change from one thing into another, for example from one energy type into another

crude oil fossil fuel found in seabeds formed from sea creatures and plants millions of years ago

electric current controlled flow of electrons around a circuit

extract take out of the ground

flammable catches fire easily

fossil fuels fuels made from the ancient remains of plants and animals

fracking slang for hydraulic fracturing, the process of extracting gas and oil by using a pressurized fluid to increase fractures or tears in underground rock layers

fuel material that is burned or used to produce power

generator machine that turns mechanical energy into electrical energy

geologist someone who studies the structure of Earth

global warming gradual rise in the temperature of Earth's atmosphere

greenhouse gas gas that traps heat in Earth's atmosphere

import bring in from other countries

irreversable something that cannot be changed

magnify enlarge

matter substances

methane colourless, odourless greenhouse gas that is highly flammable

NASA short for National Aeronautics and Space Administration, the US government agency responsible for space exploration

non-renewable describes an energy source that will eventually run out – for example coal, oil and gas

nuclear fission splitting of the nucleus of a uranium atom into two or more nuclei

nucleus centre of an atom

odourless without smell

organic natural

photon particle of electomagnetic radiation such as light

photosynthesis process that plants use to make food using the energy from sunlight

power station place where a lot of energy is produced and then sent to where it is needed

radiation energy that travels in electromagnetic waves

refinery place where energy resources, such as crude oil, are refined and made ready for use

renewable energy energy that comes from natural sources and can be replaced

rotor spinning blade

thermal energy energy from heat

turbine wheel or motor driven by steam, water or air

wave way some energy travels

Find out more

Books

DK Findout! Energy, Emily Dodd (DK Children, 2018)

Energy (Essential Physical Science), Louise and Richard Spilsbury (Raintree 2014)

From Crude Oil to Fast Food Snacks: An energy journey through the world of heat (Energy Journeys), Ian Graham (Raintree, 2016)

Science vs the Energy Crisis (Science Fights Back), Nick Hunter (Raintree, 2017)

Websites

www.bbc.com/bitesize/articles/ztxwqty
Learn more about renewable and non-renewable energy.

www.dkfindout.com/uk/science/energy
Find out more about energy.

Index